TAKE A
BALL *of*
STRING

16 BEAUTIFUL PROJECTS FOR YOUR HOME

TAKE A
BALL of
STRING

16 BEAUTIFUL PROJECTS FOR YOUR HOME

Jemima Schlee

First published 2015 by
Guild of Master Craftsman Publications Ltd
Castle Place, 166 High Street, Lewes,
East Sussex BN7 1XU

Text © Jemima Schlee, 2015

Copyright in the Work © GMC Publications Ltd, 2015

ISBN 978 1 86108 793 5

Publisher Jonathan Bailey
Production Manager Jim Bulley
Senior Project Editor Virginia Brehaut
Editor Alison Howard
Managing Art Editor Gilda Pacitti
Photographer Andrew Perris
Art Editor Luana Gobbo
Step Photography Jemima Schlee and Martha Bamford

Colour origination by GMC Reprographics
Printed and bound in China

For Harrison and Martha

Contents

Kitchen Cloths p.36

Dish Scrubs p.32

Coin Purse p.76

Tablet Cover p.58

Desk Trays p.50

Pebble Doorstop p.64

First-aid Purse p.94

Storage Boxes p.90

Bath Mat p.86

INTRODUCTION

This is not a book about brown paper packages tied up with string, it is far more than that. Here are 16 useful and beautiful items that can be woven, crocheted and knitted from a humble ball of string.

STRING HAS A LONG and interesting history. It was made and used by the Egyptians as long ago as 4,000BCE. It has been made from grass, paper, hair and hide and has been used to pull, tie, carry and connect. Despite the introduction of machine technology and man-made materials, the way in which string, cord and rope is made today remains basically unchanged. String can be bought in an amazing variety of textures, weights and colours, from candy-striped bakers' twine to soft, hollow-braid cotton cord or rope.

Most of the projects in this book are made from standard twine or household string that knits or crochets to the same tension as double knitting cotton. Some also use a thicker cotton cord or rope for a chunkier result.

Tension is only crucial in a few of the projects, so you don't need to worry about it too much. If you can't find string in a colour you like, dye your own natural-fibred string in a solid colour, or dip dye your finished work to create an ombré tonal effect.

This page: Coasters **page 28**
Opposite: Dish Scrubs **page 32**

This page:
Kitchen Cloths
page 36
Opposite:
Pot Holders
page 40

Opposite: Circular Rug **page 46**
This page: Desk Trays **page 50**

This page: Lampshade **page 54**
Opposite: Tablet Cover **page 58**

Opposite:
Pebble Doorstop **page 64**
This page:
Jam-jar Candleholder **page 68**

This page: Wash Mitts **page 82**
Opposite: Bath Mat **page 86**

This page:
Storage Boxes **page 90**
Opposite:
First-aid Purse **page 94**

THE KITCHEN

Protect tabletops from glass and cup rings using these coasters, which also make an ideal gift. When you get into the rhythm of this relatively easy pattern, try making larger, rectangular place mats. This is a great project for using up scraps of string.

COASTERS

Supplies:
For each coaster

- ☐ 25yds (23m) bakers' twine or household string, for outer edge (A)
- ☐ 6yds (5.5m) bakers' twine or household string, for central square (B)
- ☐ 5mm (UK6:USH/8) crochet hook
- ☐ 3mm (UK11:US-) crochet hook or large darning needle to finish off ends
- ☐ Steam iron
- ☐ Sharp scissors
- ☐ Liquid starch or cornstarch (optional)

Size:
Approximately 4¼in (11cm) square

Tension:
Not crucial, but the example was worked to a tension of 4dc x 4 rows to 1in (2.5cm) square.

COASTER

Using the 5mm hook and A, make a slip knot and work 18ch, turn.

Row 1: Using A, dc into second ch from hook, dc into each of next 16ch, 1ch, turn.

Rows 2–5: Using A, dc into second dc of previous row, work 15dc placing last dc in turning ch of previous row (17dc including turning ch), 1ch, turn.

Rows 6–13: Using A, dc into second dc, work 3dc changing to B in last dc; work 7dc in B changing to A in last dc; work 5dc using A.

When changing from A to B, work up to the last stitch using A **1**.

For the final wrap, drop A and use B for the last pull through **2** so the loop on the hook is in B, ready to work the first full stitch **3**.

Work the given number of sts in B until the last stitch **4**.

On the final wrap of the last stitch, drop B and use A for the last pull through **5**.

Continue in A to end **6**.

Row 14: Using A, dc into second dc, work 5dc, cut B leaving a 2in (5cm) tail, continue in A to end, 1ch, turn.

Rows 15–17: Using A, dc into second dc, dc to end, 1ch, turn **7**.

Note: cut the second A string as you pass it, leaving a 2in (5cm) tail.

Row 18: Using A, dc into second dc, dc to end. Cut A, leaving a 2in (5cm) tail. Pull the tail through the last ch and pull tight to finish **8**.

FINISHING OFF

Finish off all ends using a darning needle or small crochet hook to run them through several stitches at the back of the work. Cut the string flush. If desired, spray or soak the coaster with starch (see page 52); press using a steam iron.

TIP

AS YOU WORK ROWS 2–5, YOU CAN CROCHET IN THE CASTING-ON TAIL OF COLOUR B.

See also:
Double crochet *page 107*
Working turning chains *page 108*
Changing colour *page 110*

1

2

3

4

5

6

7

8

These great little scrubs will jolly up the dish-washing and, once you've mastered the simple pattern, you won't be able to stop at just one. They make great gifts and look wonderful made in an array of different colours.

DISH SCRUBS

Supplies:
For each dish scrub

- [ ] 35yds (32m) polypropylene twine
- [ ] 4.5mm (UK7:US7) crochet hook
- [ ] Sharp scissors

Size:
Approximately 3½in (9cm) in diameter

Tension:
Not crucial

FIRST SIDE

Work 6ch, sl st into first st of ch to form a ring **1**.

Round 1: 3ch (to form first tr), 11tr into ring, sl st into third st of 3ch (12 sts) **2**.

Round 2: Sl st into next st, 3ch (to form first tr), 1tr into base of 3ch, 2tr into next and each of following 10 sts, sl st into third st of 3ch (24 sts).

Round 3: 1ch (to form first dc), dc into each of next 23 sts (24 sts).

Note: your work will curve slightly on the last round.

Round 4: Sl st into next st, 3ch (to form first tr), 1tr into base of 3ch, 1tr into next st, *2tr into next st, 1tr into next st, rep from * 10 times more, sl st into third st of 3ch (36 sts).

Cut twine to 4in (10cm) and pull the tail end through the last st **3**.

SECOND SIDE

Make another side in exactly the same way, but do not cut the twine at the end of Round 4. It will be used to join the two halves.

JOINING THE HALVES

Place the crochet discs wrong sides together and join using dc. Do this by pushing the hook through the first stitch of each half, then working the dc as normal. Work each corresponding stitch in turn in the same way **4**.

FINISHING OFF

Cut twine to 4in (10cm) and pull the tail through the last stitch. Using the hook, work the remaining length of twine through the spaces between the two sides of the scrub **5**.

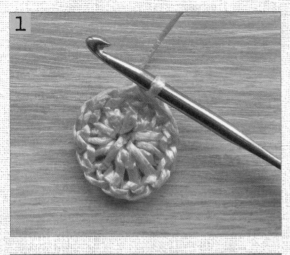

See also:
Double crochet *page 107*
Treble crochet *page 109*
Working in the round *page 112*
Increasing *page 111*

Classic hand-knitted cloths in subtle stripes and checks make a stylish addition to your kitchen. Change the tones and colours to make contrasting designs. They are so fast and satisfying to work that you may find it hard to stop making them!

KITCHEN CLOTHS

Supplies:

- [ ] 90yds (83m) neutral household string (A)
- [ ] Red perlé embroidery cotton (B): 72yds (66m) for striped cloth 30yds (28m) for checked cloth
- [ ] 3mm (UK11:US-) knitting needles
- [ ] Small crochet hook or darning needle to finish off ends
- [ ] Sharp scissors

Size:

Approximately 9½in (24cm) square

Tension:

Not crucial, but the example was worked to a tension of 4 sts x 7 rows in moss st to 1in (2.5cm) square.

PATTERN NOTES

The cloths are worked in moss stitch and the stripes or checks are formed by adding a strand of B and knitting it together with A **1**. Leave a 4in (10cm) tail of B at the beginning and end of each stripe or check.

PLAIN CLOTH **2**

Using A, cast on 37 sts.
Row 1: K1, (p1, k1) to end.
Row 2: Sl1 purl-wise, (p1, k1) to end.
These two rows form the moss-stitch pattern.
Work 54 rows in total.
Cast off loosely in moss stitch.

STRIPED CLOTH **3**

Using A, cast on 37 sts.
Rows 1–5: Work in moss st using A only.
Rows 6–11: Work in moss st using A and B held together.
Rep rows 1–11 until four horizontal stripes have been completed.
Cut B leaving a 4in (10cm) tail.
Rows 48–53: Work in moss st using A only.
Row 54: Cast off in moss st.
Weave in the ends invisibly using a darning needle or small crochet hook, then cut the ends off flush.

CHECKED CLOTH **4**

Wind off four individual small balls of B, which will be used in turn for the vertical stripes. Use a separate ball for each stripe and do not carry it across the back of the work. The remainder will be used for the horizontal stripes.
Using A, cast on 37 sts.
Rows 1–5: Working in moss st throughout, work 4 sts using A only; * work 1 st holding together a strand of A and a strand of B from one of the small balls; work 6 sts using A only, rep from * until 5 sts remain, work 1 st holding together A and B from the final ball; work 4 sts using A only.
Row 6: Work across row in moss st using A and B held together.
Rows 7–16: Work 4 sts using A only; * work 1 st using A and B, work 6 sts using A only, rep from * until 5 sts remain, work 1 st using A and B, work 4 sts using A only.
Row 17: Work using A and B held together.
Rep rows 7–17 until four horizontal stripes have been completed.
Rows 51–55: Work 4 sts using A only; * work 1 st using A and B, work 6 sts using A only, rep from * until 5 sts remain, work 1 st using A and B, work 4 sts using A only.
Rows 56: Cast off in moss st.
Finish off ends using a darning needle or a small crochet hook to weave them invisibly through the work, then cut them off flush.

TIP

MULTI-COLOURED STRIPES AND
CHECKS ALSO LOOK GREAT AND USE
UP SMALL SCRAPS OF THREAD.

See also:
Moss stitch *page 117*
Working blocks of colour *page 120*

These generously sized pot holders are invaluable for saving burnt fingers and can also be used as mats to protect your tabletops. The 'tumbling block' pattern is taken from a traditional design found in Ancient Greek and Roman mosaics.

POT HOLDERS

Supplies:
For each pot holder

- [ ] 70yds (64m) medium tone (grey) bakers' twine or household string (A)
- [ ] 60yds (55m) light tone (neutral) bakers' twine or household string (B)
- [ ] 45yds (42m) dark tone (red) bakers' twine or household string (C)
- [ ] 4mm (UK8:USG/6) crochet hook
- [ ] Cotton embroidery thread in a neutral shade
- [ ] 2.5mm (UK12:USC/2) crochet hook or large darning needle to finish off ends
- [ ] Sharp scissors

Size:
Approximately 12 x 10½in (30 x 26.5cm)

Tension:
Not crucial, but the example was worked to a tension of 4dc x 4 rows to 1in (2.5cm) square.

SPECIAL INSTRUCTION:
DEC1
Insert hook in next ch or dc and draw a loop through; insert hook in foll ch or dc and draw a loop through, wrap yarn and draw through three loops.

ZIGZAG STRIP 1 (MAKE 2)

Using the 4mm hook and A, make 13ch.

Row 1: Dc in third ch from hook, dc in each of next 8 ch, dec1 in dc over next 2 ch, 2ch, turn.

Row 2: Dc in second dc, dc in each of next 8 dc, dc in turning chain of previous row, 2ch, turn.

Row 3: Dc in first dc, dc in each of next 8 dc, dec1 in dc over next dc and turning ch, 2ch, turn.

Rows 4 and 6: As row 2.

Rows 5 and 7: As row 3.

Row 8: Dc in second dc, dc in each of next 8 dc, dc in turning ch.

Change to B, 2ch, turn (one lozenge made) .

Row 9: Dc in second dc, dc in each of the next 8 dc, dc in turning ch, 2ch, turn .

Row 10: Dc in first dc, dc in each of next 8 dc, dec1 over next dc and turning ch of previous row, 2ch, turn.

Row 11: Dc in second dc, dc in each of the next 8 dc, dc in turning ch of previous row, 2ch, turn.

Row 12: As row 10.

Row 13: As row 11.

Row 14: As row 10.

Row 15: As row 11.

Row 16: As row 10.

Row 17: Dc in second dc, dc in each of next 8 dc, dc in turning ch of previous row changing to A in last st, 2ch, turn .

Row 18: Using A, dc in second dc, dc in each of next 8 dc, dc in turning ch, 2ch, turn.

Row 19: Dc in first dc, dc in each of next 8 dc, dec1 over next st and turning chain of previous row, 2ch, turn.

Continue like this, changing colour appropriately until five sections have been made (three A and two B).

Final row: Dc in second dc, dc in each of next 8 dc, dec1 over next st and turning ch.

Cut string leaving a 4in (10cm) tail. Pull through loop on hook to finish off .

ZIGZAG STRIP 2 (MAKE 1)

Using the 4mm crochet hook and B, make 13ch.

Work as for zigzag strip 1 but making three B and two A sections.

You should now have three zigzag strips – 2 of strip 1 and 1 of strip 2 .

DIAMONDS (MAKE 4)

Using C, make 13ch.

Work rows 1–7 of zigzag strip 1.

Row 8: Dc in second dc, dc in each of next 8 dc, dc in turning ch.

Cut string leaving a 4in (5cm) tail and pull through loop on hook to finish.

TRIANGLES (MAKE 2)

Row 1: Using the 4mm crochet hook and C, make 13ch.

Row 2: Dc in third ch from hook, dc over each of the next 8ch, dec1 over next 2 ch, 2ch, turn.

Row 3: Dc in second dc, dc over each of the next 6 dc, dec1 over next dc and turning ch, 2ch, turn.

Row 4: Dc in second dc, dc over each of the next 5 dc, dec1 over next dc and turning ch, 2ch, turn.

Row 5: Dc in second dc, dc over each of the next 4 dc, dec1 over next dc and turning ch, 2ch, turn.

Row 6: Dc in second dc, dc over each of the next 3 dc, dec1 over next dc and turning ch, 2ch, turn.

Row 7: Dc in second dc, dc over each of the next 2 dc, dec1 over next dc and turning ch, 2ch, turn.

Row 8: Dc in second dc, dec1 over next dc and turning ch, 2ch, turn.

Row 9: Dec1 over second dc and turning ch.

Cut string leaving a 4in (5cm) tail and pull through loop on hook to finish off .

MAKING UP

Assemble the three strips, four diamonds and two triangles following the photo **7** and sew together from the back using neutral thread. Using the small crochet hook or large darning needle, finish off the string ends by hooking them through stitches at the back of the work. Trim ends flush.

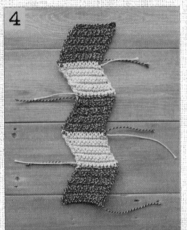

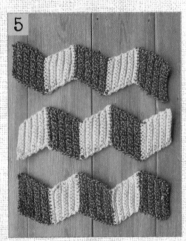

THE OFFICE

This dappled rug made with cotton rope and string is based on a wonderful African basket-making technique, and is a great project for using up scraps. It can be made to any size, but be warned: the larger it becomes, the more slowly it grows!

CIRCULAR RUG

Supplies:

- ☐ 50yds (46m) cord/rope approximately ⅜in (1cm) in diameter
- ☐ 300yds (275m) bakers' twine or household string made up of various lengths in several colours
- ☐ Large darning needle
- ☐ Sewing machine
- ☐ Sewing needle and sewing cotton
- ☐ Steam iron
- ☐ Sharp scissors

Size:

Approximately 34in (86cm) diameter

Step 1

Flatten the end of the cord/rope slightly with your fingers and use a sewing machine to zigzag stitch back and forth across its width 1in (2.5cm) from the end. Trim with sharp scissors to prevent the softly woven cord from fraying.

Step 2

Thread the darning needle with a 2yd (2m) length of string and knot one end. Begin coiling the rope, positioning the zigzag-stitched end beneath and to the back. Working from the front and holding the curl of rope in place between your thumb and finger, pull the needle through the centre from the back and make a stitch to hold the first two rounds together.

Step 3

Join each spiralling round of rope by attaching it to the previous round with a figure-of-eight-shaped wrap.

Step 4

To change colour or begin a new length of string, turn the work over and feed the end of the previous length of string back through the rope coil for about 2in (5cm) to hide it.

Step 5

When you pull the needle out again, trim the string flush with the surface of the rope.

TIP

KEEP YOUR WORK AS FLAT AS POSSIBLE AS IT 'GROWS'. IF IT BEGINS TO CURL THERE SHOULD BE NO NEED TO UNDO YOUR PREVIOUS WORK; JUST SLACKEN THE ROPE SLIGHTLY AS YOU CONTINUE TO STITCH. WHEN COMPLETE, PRESS VERY FIRMLY USING A HOT STEAM IRON AND LEAVE IT UNDER A HEAVY BOARD TO FLATTEN IT.

Step 6

Begin a new length of string by running it through the rope for approximately 2in (5cm) before starting to wrap the figures-of-eight. Continue working in a spiral, changing colours randomly as you go.

Step 7

To finish, flatten the end of the rope with your fingers and zigzag stitch back and forth across it using a sewing machine. Bend it so that the end is tucked and hidden at the back. Use a needle threaded double with sewing cotton and anchor it to the reverse of your work by overstitching.

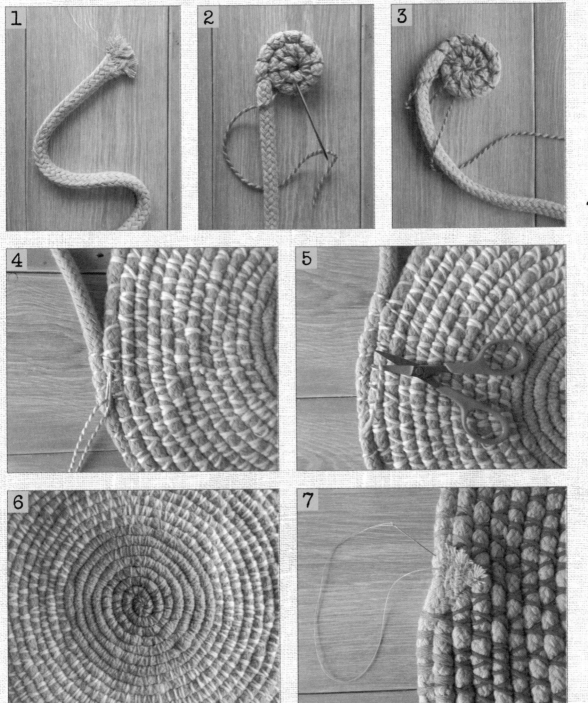

These shallow trays will help to keep all your bits and bobs in order. Paperclips, pens, postage stamps and other stationery items can be corralled and tidied away. This design is very easy to adapt to produce different shapes and sizes.

DESK TRAYS

Supplies:

For the medium tray:

☐ 35yds (32m) bakers' twine or household string in white (A)

☐ 2yds (2m) contrasting bakers' twine or household string

For the small square tray

☐ 30yds (28m) bakers' twine or household string in black (B)

☐ 2yds (2m) contrasting bakers' twine or household string

For the large tray:

☐ 65yds (60m) bakers' twine or household string in grey (C)

☐ 3yds (3m) contrasting bakers' twine or household string

For all trays:

☐ 3.5mm (UK9:USE/4) crochet hook

☐ Liquid starch or cornstarch

☐ Large darning needle

☐ *Sharp scissors*

Sizes:

Medium tray: approximately 4 x 2½ x 1in (10 x 6 x 2.5cm)
Small square tray: approximately 3 x 2½ x 1in (7.5 x 6 x 2.5cm)
Large tray: approximately 7 x 2½ x 1in (18 x 6 x 2.5cm)

Tension:

Approximately 10dc x 10 rows to 1in (2.5cm).

MEDIUM TRAY

Using A, make 20ch, turn.

Rows 1–11: Dc into second ch from hook, dc to end, 1ch, turn.

Row 12: Dc into second ch from hook, dc to end. Turn **1**.

Row 13: Continuing in dc, work the next row through the front thread of each st from the row below to begin the sides and form a corner **2**.

Row 14: Pick up and work 15dc along the next edge, 20dc along the third edge and 15 dc from the final edge (70 sts in total) **3**.

Row 15: Join with a sl st to first dc, make 1ch, dc to end.

Rep last row 3 times more.

Fasten off. Cut the string to 4in (10cm) and pull it through the last loop on the hook **4**.

SMALL SQUARE TRAY

Using B, make 15ch, turn.

Rows 1–11: Dc into second ch from hook to end, 1ch, turn.

Row 12: Dc into second ch from hook to end, turn.

Row 13: Continuing in dc, work the next row through the front thread only of each stitch to begin the sides and form the corners. Pick up and work 15dc along each of the next three sides (60 sts). Work 4 rounds of dc.

Cut string to 4in (10cm) and pull through the last loop on the hook.

LARGE TRAY

Using C, make 35ch, turn.

Rows 1–11: Dc into second ch from hook to end, 1ch, turn.

Row 12: Dc into second ch from hook, dc in each dc to end working last st into turning ch of previous row, 1ch, turn.

Row 13: Continuing in dc, work the next row through the front thread of each st from the row below to start the sides and form a corner. Pick up and work 15dc along the next side, 35dc along the third side and 15dc along the last side (100 sts). Work Row 15 of the medium tray and then rep 3 times more.

Cut string to 4in (10cm) and pull through the last loop on the hook.

TOP EDGE DETAIL (ALL TRAYS)

Using a length of contrasting string threaded on a large darning needle, run through several stitches just below the top row of crochet stitches halfway along one edge of the tray **5**. Work around the top edge by overstitching, working through every second stitch **6**. To finish off, run the needle through several stitches just below the top row. Cut thread flush using sharp scissors. Finish off the thread tails using the needle or a small crochet hook **7**.

STARCHING THE TRAYS

Use liquid starch or make your own by mixing a heaped teaspoon of cornstarch into approximately ¼ cup of water at room temperature and stir until completely dissolved. Add 1¾ cups of boiling water and leave to cool to room temperature before pouring it into a spray bottle. Saturate the finished work with the starch. Tease, pull and manipulate the sides to straighten them and push out the corners to make them sharp. Leave the work on a towel to dry.

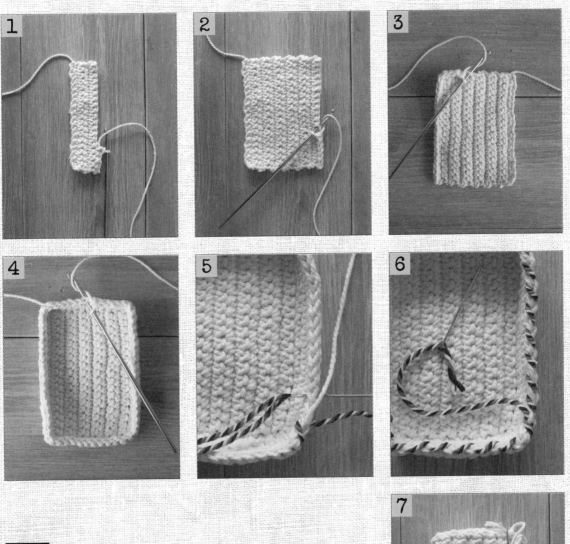

TIP

THESE LITTLE TRAYS ARE ALSO PERFECT FOR
KEEPING RINGS AND EARRINGS ORGANIZED.

Transform a plain lampshade for your work desk using different colours and combinations of string to create contrasting tonal and speckled effects. The light will be softened through the shade, and cast down onto your work.

LAMPSHADE

Supplies:
- [ ] 630yds (576m) bakers' twine or household string made up from lengths in various colours
- [ ] Lampshade
- [ ] PVA adhesive and brush or glue gun
- [ ] Sharp scissors
- [ ] Darning needle
- [ ] Damp cloth

Size:
To fit a lampshade measuring 7in (18cm) diameter x 25in (64cm) high

Step 1

Prepare the materials before you begin. If using PVA, pour it into a bowl, add a tiny amount of water to make it easier to spread and mix to a smooth consistency using the brush. If using a glue gun, switch it on and follow the manufacturer's instructions. The hot glue dries quickly and the flow can be tricky to control so, if you are unfamiliar with the technique, practise first by attaching string to a scrap of card.

Step 2

Beginning at the back of the shade by the seam, spread adhesive along about 2in (5cm) of the lower edge. Flatten the end of the string and use the brush to paste it to the fabric of the shade so it curves up away from the lower edge.

Step 3

Continue to apply adhesive along the lower edge of the shade, positioning the string neatly round the base and applying pressure so that it adheres to the surface. As you complete each circumference, the working end of the string should cover the raw end neatly. Keeping the surface prepared with adhesive, continue winding string round the shade and applying pressure, so the rows lie snugly against each other and are firmly attached.

Step 4

It is best to add or change colours on the seam at the back of the lampshade. To do this, drop the existing colour and flatten the end of the string in the new colour against the surface of the shade. Continue to curve up and away from the lower edge as with for the foundation row.

Step 5

Continue to apply the adhesive and position the string, both strands together, which makes progress fairly swift.

Step 6

At each colour change, cut the existing string about ⅜in (1cm) beyond the seam of the shade, flattening it and gluing it down. Do exactly the same with the new colour, overlapping it with the previous colour.

Step 7

Continue all the way up the shade, mixing and combining string to create your unique design. On the final round, cut the string ⅜in (1cm) beyond the seam and use a darning needle to poke the raw end down behind the string of the previous row. Use a damp cloth to wipe any excess adhesive from the top rim of the shade.

TIP

WORK OUT YOUR DESIGN AND COLOUR DISTRIBUTION BEFORE YOU START. COVER A STRIP OF CARD 3IN (7.5CM) X THE HEIGHT OF THE LAMPSHADE WITH DOUBLE-SIDED TAPE. CUT 3IN (7.5CM) LENGTHS OF STRING AND STICK THEM TO THE CARD TO CREATE YOUR DESIGN. REMOVE AND REARRANGE THEM AS YOU WISH.

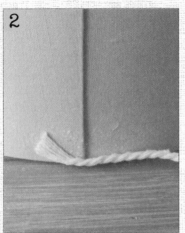

This utilitarian cover knitted in string has a contrasting leather buckle and is great for protecting your tablet from scratches and knocks. You could make a much larger one for a laptop and use two buckles to fasten it.

TABLET COVER

Supplies:
- [ ] 100yds (915m) bakers' twine or household string for the mini size; 150yds (138m) for the standard size
- [ ] 4mm (UK8:US6) knitting needles
- [ ] Small crochet hook or large darning needle to finish off ends
- [ ] Leather buckle
- [ ] Waxed linen thread
- [ ] Sewing needle and pins
- [ ] Sewing machine
- [ ] Steam iron
- [ ] Sharp scissors

Size:
To fit a mini tablet measuring approximately 8 x 5¼ x⅓in (200 x 135 x 7.5mm) [standard tablet measuring approximately 9½ x 6½ x⅓in (240 x 170 x 7.5mm)]

Tension:
4 sts x 6 rows to 1in (2.5cm) square, in stocking stitch using 4mm needles. The cover should be a snug fit, so it is important to check tension.

MAIN PIECE

Using 4mm needles, cast on 24[32] sts.

Work 92[100] rows in stocking stitch.

Decrease row: K2tog tbl, k to last 2 sts,
k2tog (22[30] sts).

Next row: Sl1, knit to end.

Rep last row 20 times.

Final row: Skpo, cast off 20[28] sts, sl last st onto
right needle, pass st on right over the sl st, cut string
to 4in (10cm) and use a needle or small crochet
hook to thread the tail through a few stitches before
cutting flush. Press work using a hot iron. Finish off
any ends using a large darning needle or a small
crochet hook **1**.

MAKING UP

Lay the work out, right side up and with the cast-on
edge nearest you. Fold the lower edge up to align
with the decrease row. Pin the edges together with
right sides facing and join using a sewing machine
or by hand **2**. Turn the cover the right side out. Slip
the tablet into the case to check fit **3**. Fold the flap
down snugly and pin the buckle in place **4**.

FINISHING OFF

Undo buckle and sew both halves in place using
waxed thread and a needle **5**. Work all the way
round the leather buckle pieces with the waxed
thread using running stitch. Turn and continue to
stitch around the buckle once more, so that your
stitches fill the gaps. It's also a good idea to sew
double stitches on either side where the buckle
pieces join just to give extra strength.

TIP

IF YOU WANT TO MAKE A COVER FOR
A LAPTOP, DRAW A PAPER PATTERN
AND USE YOUR TENSION SQUARE
TO WORK OUT HOW MANY STITCHES
YOU NEED TO CAST ON. CHECK THE
KNITTING AGAINST THE LAPTOP AS
YOU PROGRESS, TO CALCULATE WHEN
TO WORK THE DECREASE ROW.

See also:
Stocking stitch *page 117*
Decreasing *page 119*
Sewn seams *page 123*

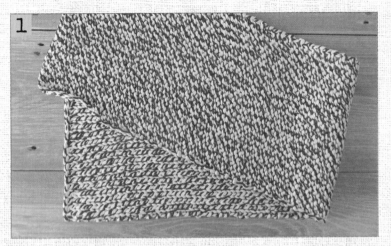

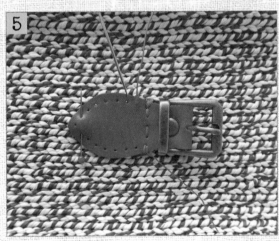

THE PORCH

This simple doorstop was inspired by an old fishing net and uses a Turkish stitch pattern to recreate the fluid, knotted structure. The little bag can be filled with pebbles and used to keep your door ajar, allowing a cool breeze to blow through your home on summer evenings.

PEBBLE DOORSTOP

Supplies:
- [ ] 70yds (64m) of bakers' twine
- [ ] 5mm (UK6:US8) circular knitting needle
- [ ] 5mm (UK6:US8) double-pointed knitting needles
- [ ] Large darning needle
- [ ] Sharp scissors
- [ ] Pebbles
- [ ] Scraps of string or safety pins for markers

Size:
Approximately 8in (20cm) diameter when empty

Tension:
Not crucial, but the example was worked to a tension of 4 sts x 4 rows to 1in (2.5cm) square.

THE BASE

Using 5mm circular needles, cast on 15 sts.
Working back and forth as with regular needles,
work 17 rows in moss stitch thus:

Row 1: K1, (p1, k1) to end.

Rows 2–17: Sl1 purlwise, (p1, k1) to end 1.

Row 18: Continuing from the end of the last row,
pick up and knit 15 sts along each of the other three
sides of the square (total 60 sts). Place a marker at
this point using a scrap of string or a safety pin to
mark the beginning of the rounds you will now be
working in 2.

TURKISH STITCH PATTERN

Round 1: (K2tog, yon) to end.

Round 2: (Yon, k2tog) to end.

Repeat this two-row pattern 9 times more. On odd
rounds, there will be a 'yon' on either side of the
marker at the changeover, and on even rounds
there will be a 'k2tog' on either side of the marker.
As you work, check that the stitch of each round
slants in the opposite direction from the stitch in
the round below, forming a zigzag 3.

Decrease round for top row: (K2tog) to end.
Cast off until 1 st remains on the needle 4.

See also:
Moss stitch *page 117*
Increasing *page 118*
Decreasing *page 119*
Joined-on i-cord *page 124*
Grafting *page 122*

TIP

YOU CAN MAKE THE DOORSTOP
LARGER OR SMALLER BY INCREASING
OR DECREASING THE NUMBER OF
ROWS KNITTED IN THE TURKISH
STITCH PATTERN.

NECK-EDGE I-CORD

Change to double-pointed needles and cast on
3 sts (4 sts on needle) 5.

*K3, sl1, pick up 1 st from cast off edge, psso, rep
from * until all cast-off sts have been worked.
Cast off leaving a 12in (30cm) tail 6.

FINISHING OFF

Thread the tail on a darning needle and join the
two ends of the i-cord. For an invisible join, graft by
weaving the string through the first and last rows of
stitching following the rhythm of the stocking stitch.
Fill the bag with pebbles and draw up the i-cord 7.

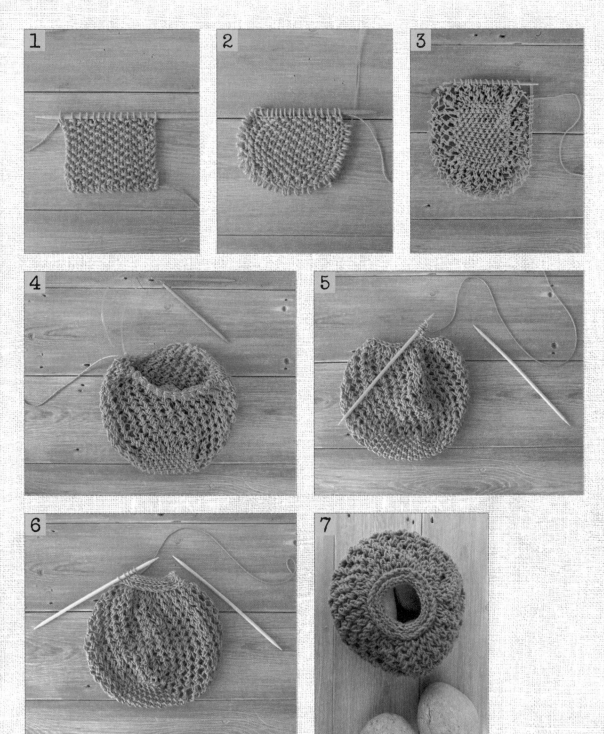

Light up your porch or pathway, dining table or windowsill
with these little candleholders made from jam jars.
They are ombré dyed to complement the flickering light
and have little loops for hanging.

JAM-JAR CANDLEHOLDER

Supplies:
- [ ] 20–25yds (19–21m) bakers' twine or household string
- [ ] 4.5mm (UK7:US7) crochet hook
- [ ] Fabric dye
- [ ] Salt (read dye instructions for quantity)
- [ ] Glass bowl or jug
- [ ] Pebbles
- [ ] Sharp scissors

Size:
To fit a 1lb (16oz) jam jar, measuring 3in (7.5cm) diameter x 4½in (11.5cm) high

Tension:
Not crucial – this pattern 'grows' round the jar as you work and can be adjusted to accommodate variations in size.

WARNING
Never leave candles unattended.

JAM-JAR CANDLEHOLDER

Work 6ch and join with a sl st to form a ring.

Round 1: 3ch, 11tr into ring, sl st into third of 3ch █1.

Round 2: 4ch, *1tr into next st, 1ch, rep from * 10 times more, sl st into third of 4ch to complete the round █2.

Round 3: Sl st into each of next 2 sts, 5ch, *1tr into the ch between the next 2 trebles on the previous round, 2ch, rep from * 10 times more (11 times in total), sl st into third of 5ch to complete the round. Repeat round 3 until work is required length (measurement A on diagram).

Final round: 4ch, *1tr into next st, 1ch, rep from * 10 times more but do not fasten off. Turn jar upside down and ease work over it – it may be a tight fit, but persevere. Once on, ease the top line of sts into the neck of the jar (B), then sl st into the third of the 4ch to complete, but do not fasten off █3.

HANGING LOOP

Work 20ch, sl st into the first ch, cut string to 4in (10cm) and hook through the final loop. Use a small hook to work in the tail end of the string and finally cut it flush to the jar █4.

OMBRÉ DYEING

Dye work following the instructions below, placing several pebbles inside to weigh it down during the process and prevent irregular colouring.

Step A

Assemble all necessary equipment near a sink. Using a large glass bowl or jug make a strong dye solution; I used quarter of a pack of dye, a quarter of the specified quantity of salt and 4fl oz (100ml) of hot water. As you work through the process you will be diluting the solution and therefore lightening the colour of your dye.

Step B

Stir the strong dye solution thoroughly before placing the work in it. Dyes usually take better on damp fibres, so dampen the work before immersing it in the dye.

Step C

After 10 minutes, add 100ml of hot water to the dye, taking care not to splash colour on your work. Wait 10 minutes, then add another 100ml of water.

Step D

10 minutes later, add a further 100ml of hot water to the jug. Leave for 10 minutes to complete the dyeing process.

Step E

When you are satisfied with the effect, rinse work under cool, then warm running water until it runs clear. Set aside to dry.

1

2

3

4

TIP

AS AN ALTERNATIVE,
YOU CAN MAKE THESE
IN COLOURED STRING
OR IN STRIPES AND
THEN LEAVE OUT
THE FINAL DYEING
PROCESS.

A

B

C

D

E

This traditional string bag expands to become unexpectedly capacious as you fill it. As a bonus, it has a more closely knitted lower section so small items won't fall through the bottom and get lost.

MARKET BAG

Supplies:
- ☐ 100yds (92m) blue/white butchers' twine (A)
- ☐ 200yds (183m) orange/white butchers' twine (B)
- ☐ 5mm (UK6:U8) circular knitting needle
- ☐ 5mm (UK6:U8) double-pointed knitting needles
- ☐ Sharp scissors
- ☐ Large darning needle
- ☐ Scraps of string or safety pins for markers

Size:
Approximately 12in (30cm) square when empty

Tension:
Not crucial, but the example was worked to a tension of 4 sts x 4 rows to 1in (2.5cm) square, measured over pattern.

MAIN PIECE

Using 5mm circular knitting needles and A,
cast on 46 sts.

Pattern 1

Row 1: Purl to end.

Row 2: K1, *yon, k2tog, rep from * to end.

Row 3: Purl to end.

Row 4: *Skpo, rep from * to last st, k1.

These four rows form the pattern for the A section.
Repeat them 7 times more (8 repeats in all) **1**.
Change to B.

Pattern 2

Row 1: Purl to end.

Row 2: K to end.

Row 3: Purl to end.

Row 4: *Skpo, rep from * to last st, k1.

These four rows form the pattern for the B section.
Repeat them 9 times more (10 repeats in all).
Knit 1 row.
Purl 1 row.
Change to A. Repeat Pattern 1 to work another
A section.
Cast off loosely **2**.

ASSEMBLING THE BAG

Fold work in half right sides together, aligning cast-
on and cast-off edges. Using lengths of string and
a large darning needle, join the side seams **3**.

Turn right side out and mark four points round the
open top edge of the bag using either scraps of
string or safety pins, each 2in (5cm) to either side
of the side seams.

HANDLES

Using A and 5mm double-pointed needles, work
a joined-on i-cord across each side seam between
the markers. Cast off leaving a 8in (20cm) tail.
Change to B and work a five-stitch joined-on i-cord,
beginning at the point where one of the A i-cords
finishes. Work along the edge of the bag until you
reach the beginning of the next A i-cord. Continue
working the i-cord by picking up the cast-on sts of
the A i-cord **4**.

Knit a handle by continuing in basic i-cord. Work
until handle measures 24in (61cm) then cast off
leaving a 8in (20cm) tail. Repeat for the other side
of the bag. To complete each handle, thread the
tail of B on the darning needle and join the two ends
of i-cord. Join the A and B i-cords where they meet
at the four markers **5**.

See also:

Increasing *page 118*

Decreasing *page 119*

Sewn seams *page 123*

Joined-on i-cord *page 124*

Basic i-cord *page 124*

TIP

CUSTOMIZE THIS
PATTERN TO MAKE
A SMALL SHOPPING
BAG FOR A CHILD OR A
LARGER VERSION FOR
KEEPING SCARVES,
GLOVES AND HATS ON
YOUR COAT HOOKS.

There are no dusty hidden corners in this coin purse:
the top opens wide so you won't need to scrabble about for
pennies. It's a fast, satisfying make that can easily
be adapted in size and length.

COIN PURSE

Supplies:
- [ ] 60yds (55m) bakers' twine
- [ ] 4.5mm (UK7:US7) crochet hook
- [ ] 4¼in (11cm) sew-in purse frame
- [ ] Heavy-duty waxed linen thread
- [ ] Sewing needle
- [ ] Small crochet hook or large darning needle for finishing off ends
- [ ] Four small safety pins (optional)
- [ ] Bubble wrap for stuffing
- [ ] Sharp scissors
- [ ] Liquid starch or cornstarch

Size:
4½in x 5½in (10.5cm x 14cm)

Tension:
4 dc x 4 rows to 1in (2.5cm) square. The tension is important for this project as the purse frame and crochet should have a nice snug fit.

MAKING THE HEXAGON BASE

Make 6ch and join with a sl st to make a ring.

Round 1: 1ch, 5dc into ring ■.

Round 2: Work 2dc into each of the 6 sts of the ring (12 sts). Work in the round so the piece spirals as it grows and becomes hexagonal. Place a marker at the beginning of each row, or just keep count. Each '2dc' is worked on top of the 2dc of the previous row, so after a few rows you may not need to count.

Round 3: (Dc into next st, 2dc into foll st) 6 times (18 sts).

Round 4: (Dc into each of next 2 sts, 2dc into foll st) 6 times (24 sts).

Round 5: (Dc into each of next 3 sts, 2dc into foll st) 6 times (30 sts).

Round 6: (Dc into each of next 4 sts, 2dc into foll st) 6 times (36 sts).

Round 7: (Dc into each of next 5 sts, 2dc into foll st) 6 times (42 sts).

Round 8: (Dc into each of next 6 sts, 2dc into foll st) 6 times (48 sts).

Round 9: (Dc into each of next 7 sts, 2dc into foll st) 6 times (54 sts) ■.

Open the purse frame as wide as it will go and lay it over the hexagon base. The work should be just larger than the outside edge of the frame ■. If it is too big then unravel one row. If it is too small, work another row thus:

(Dc into each of the next 8 sts, 2dc into foll st) 6 times (66 sts).

See also:

WORKING THE PURSE SIDES

Work 13 rounds in dc.

You will now have a deep bowl-shaped piece of work. Cut the string leaving a 4in (10cm) tail, then pull through the loop to finish. Weave in the tail by running it through a few stitches at the back of the work using a darning needle or small crochet hook. Cut the end flush. Using scraps of string or small safety pins, mark four points round the top rim of the work to divide it into quarters ■.

ATTACHING THE PURSE FRAME

Open out the purse frame. Starting under the clip, at the centre of one side of the frame, push the rim of the work into the frame at one of the marked points. Cut a 36in (90cm) length of waxed thread and, leaving an 18in (50cm) tail, begin to sew your work into the frame using backstitch. Work down towards one hinge, making sure the rim of the work is tucked in snugly. Stitch twice through the last two holes of the frame as you reach the hinge. Finish off the thread using a few small, tight stitches at the back of the work. Cut the thread flush ■.

Re-thread the tail at the centre point where you began stitching. Now stitch down to the other frame hinge, finishing off in the same way. Repeat for the other side of the frame. There should be a gap of about 4 sts at each hinge ■.

Manipulate the purse until you are happy with the shape. Stuff with bubble wrap, spray with starch (see page 52) and leave it to dry.

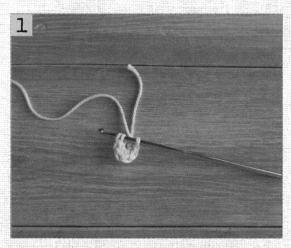

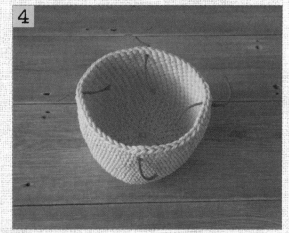

TIP

BEFORE YOU BEGIN
ATTACHING THE PURSE
FRAME, CHECK THAT
YOUR SEWING NEEDLE
FITS THROUGH THE
STITCH HOLES.

THE BATHROOM

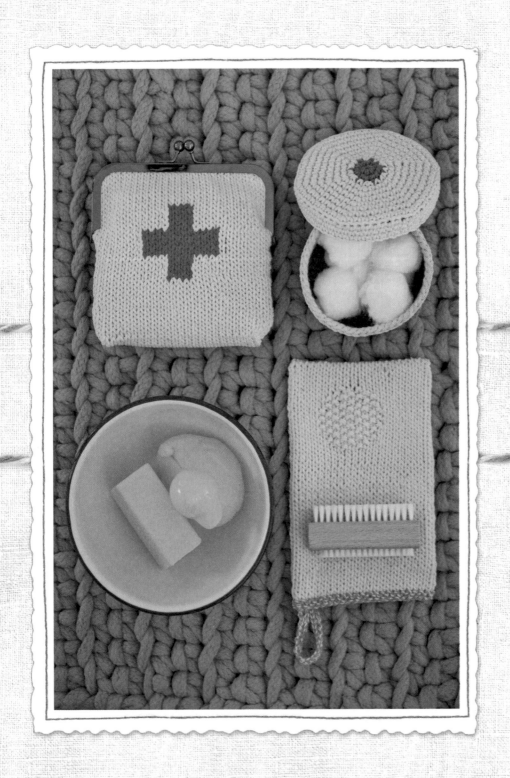

This continental version of a face flannel has a textured area for extra-effective cleansing and a little loop so you can hang it up to dry. Make different-coloured edges for each member of the family.

WASH MITTS

Supplies:

- [ ] 110yds (100m) natural-coloured bakers' twine or household string (A)
- [ ] 5yds (5m) of bakers' twine or household string in a contrasting colour (B)
- [ ] 3mm (UK11:US-) circular or double-pointed knitting needles
- [ ] Sewing needle and pins
- [ ] Sewing thread
- [ ] Sewing machine
- [ ] Darning needle
- [ ] Sharp scissors
- [ ] Steam iron

Size:

Approximately 5 x 8in (12.5 x 20cm)

Tension:

9 sts x 14 rows to 2in (5cm) square

MAIN PIECE

Using B, cast on 72 sts.

Row 1: Knit to end.

Row 2: Cast off 25 sts, k to end.

Row 3: Change to A, sl1, k to end.

Row 4: Sl1, purl to end.

The last two rows set the stocking stitch.

Continue in stocking stitch until work measures 4¾in (12cm) in length **1**.

Now work moss stitch circle using the chart below.

Row 1: Sl1, k9, p1, k1, p1, k to end.

Row 2: sl1, p32, k1, p1, k1, p1, k1, p9.

Row 3: sl1, k7, p1, k1, p1, k1, p1, k1, p1, k to end.

Row 4: sl1, p32, k1, p1, k1, p1, k1, p1, k1, p9.

Row 5: sl1, k7, p1, k1, p1, k1, p1, k1, p1, k to end.

Row 6: sl1, p30, k1, p1, k1, p1, k1, p1, k1, p1, k1, p7.

Row 7: sl1, k7, p1, k1, p1, k1, p1, k1, p1, k to end.

Row 8: sl1, p30, k1, p1, k1, p1, k1, p1, k1, p1, k1, p7.

Row 9: sl1, k7, p1, k1, p1, k1, p1, k1, p1, k to end.

Row 10: sl1, p30, k1, p1, k1, p1, k1, p1, k1, p1, k1, p7.

Row 11: sl1, k7, p1, k1, p1, k1, p1, k1, p1, k to end.

Row 12: sl1, p32, k1, p1, k1, p1, k1, p9.

Row 13: sl1, k7, p1, k1, p1, k1, p1, k1, p1, k to end.

Row 14: sl1, p32, k1, p1, k1, p1, k1, p9.

Row 15: sl1, k9, p1, k1, p1, k to end.

Work 4 rows in stocking stitch, slipping 1 st at the beginning of each row **2**.

Leave your work on the needles.

MAKING UP

Press work on the wrong side using a steam iron. With the needles still in the work, fold it in half with the wrong sides together. Thread the tail of string on a large darning needle **3**.

Hold the two knitting needles parallel, with the fold to the left and the textured panel side of the work facing, so you have a 'front' and a 'back' needle. Keep the yarn below the needles as you work. Close the top seam of the mitt using Kitchener stitch **4**.

Turn work inside out. Run the string end through the back of several stitches and cut flush. Still with the work inside out, fold the contrasting loop strip at 90 degrees so the loop falls away from the side seam. Pin or tack the two sides together from the top edge down to the contrast edge **5**. Using a fairly large stitch, machine stitch the seam, reverse stitching the bottom to add strength to the hanging loop. Finish off all ends by hand using a darning needle.

Turn the work right side out and press with a hot iron. Fold the hanging loop and use a needle and matching thread to stitch the end of it firmly to the bottom edge of the mitt **6**.

MOSS STITCH CIRCLE CHART (15 rows x 9 sts)

(Chart grid, 15 rows high × 9 stitches wide, with row markers at 5, 10, 15 on the left and stitch markers at 5 and 9 along the bottom.)

• = knit   + = purl

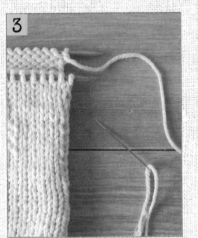

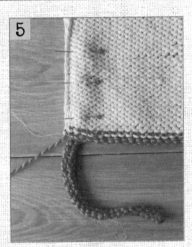

See also:

Moss stitch *page 117*

Stocking stitch *page 117*

Kitchener stitch *page 122*

Sewn seams *page 123*

Joined-on i-cord *page 124*

This gorgeous chunky bath mat is crocheted very quickly in thick cotton cord using a giant-sized hook, making it a perfect project to tackle in a day. You'll create a wonderfully textured, practical mat – and it's a simple pattern to adapt for a larger bedside rug.

BATH MAT

Supplies:
- ☐ 100yds (92m) thick cotton rope/cord, approximately ⅜in (1cm) in diameter
- ☐ 10mm (UK000:USN–P-15) crochet hook
- ☐ Sewing machine
- ☐ Sharp scissors

Size:
Approximately 27 x 16in (70 x 40cm)

Tension:
Not crucial

BATH MAT

Make 30ch **1**.

Row 1 and every following odd row: Dc into third ch from hook, dc in every ch to end to end, 2ch, turn.

Row 2 and every following even row: Working into the front loops only, dc into every dc to end, working last dc into turning ch of previous row. Work a further 14 rows or until the cord runs out (see box opposite) **2**.

To start a new length of cord, leave the last 8in (20cm) of the previous length at the back of the work. Leaving an 8in (20cm) tail, begin to use the new length. Finish the tails off at the end by hooking them through stitches at the back of the work. Cut the ends off flush **3**.

Final row: Dc into second dc, dc to end.

Cut the cord leaving an 8in (20cm) tail and pull through the loop remaining on the hook to finish **4**. Zigzag stitch across the end of the cord using a sewing machine to prevent further fraying **5**. Using the hook, pull the tail of cord through the back of several stitches to finish off **6**.

CALCULATING CORD LENGTH

To estimate roughly how much cord you need for each row, work 12 rows and turn. Fold the remaining unworked cord in four equal lengths and tie a length of string at each fold to mark the end of the first, second and third quarters. Work one more row. How many markers have you passed to work this row? If you have not reached the first marker, there will be enough cord to work a further four rows. If you have passed the first marker but not the second you may only have sufficient for two more rows.

See also:

Double crochet *page 107*
Finishing off *page 112*

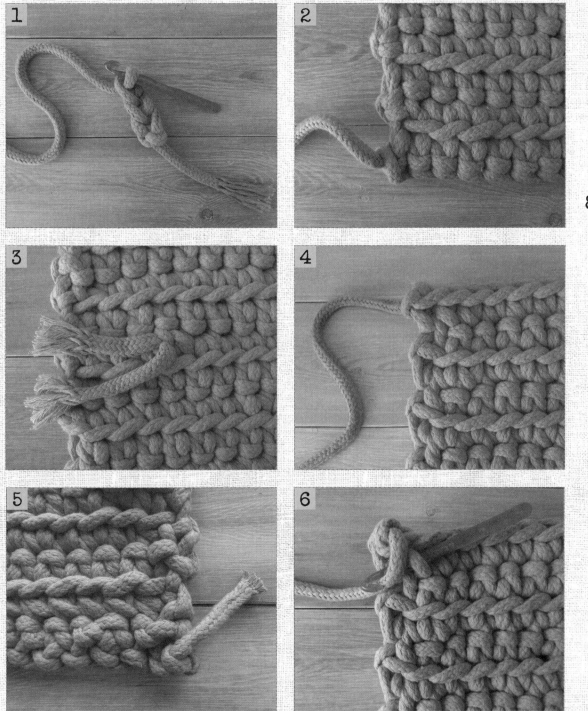

These lidded boxes are perfect for storing make-up, cotton wool, soaps and lotions. Make several and dye them to coordinate with your bathroom. Once you get the hang of the pattern, you can adjust it to make different-sized boxes.

STORAGE BOXES

Supplies:
- 75yds (69m) natural-coloured bakers' twine or household string (A)
- 2yds (2m) coloured bakers' twine or household string (B)
- 4.5mm (UK7:US7) crochet hook
- Small crochet hook or large darning needle for finishing off ends
- Fabric dye
- Salt (read dye instructions for quantity)
- Liquid starch or cornflour

Size:
Approximately 4½in (11.5cm) diameter x 3in (7cm) high

Tension:
4dc x 4 rows to 1in (2.5cm) square

TIP

THE IDEA OF DYEING YOUR WORK
CAN BE A BIT DAUNTING BECAUSE
YOU ONLY HAVE ONE GO AT IT,
BUT SEIZE THE DAY!

THE BASE

Using A, work 6ch and join with a sl st into a ring.
Round 1: Work 1ch, 5dc into ring .
Round 2: Work 2dc into each of the 6 sts of the ring.
Continue working in the round so the work spirals as it grows and slowly takes on a hexagonal shape. Place a marker at the beginning of each row if you prefer, or just keep count. The '2dc' is worked on top of the 2dc of the previous row so after a few rows you may no longer need to count.
Round 3: (1dc into next st, 2dc into following st) 6 times (18 sts).
Round 4: (Dc into each of next 2 sts, 2dc into foll st) 6 times (24 sts).
Round 5: (Dc into each of next 3 sts, 2dc into foll st) 6 times (30 sts).
Round 6: (Dc into each of next 4 sts, 2dc into foll st) 6 times (36 sts).
Round 7: (Dc into each of next 5 sts, 2dc into foll st) 6 times (42 sts).
Round 8: (Dc into each of next 6 sts, 2dc into foll st) 6 times (48 sts).
Round 9: (Dc into each of next 7 sts, 2dc into foll st) 6 times (54 sts).
(Dc into each of next 8 sts, 2dc into foll st) 6 times (60 sts) to complete the base of the box .

THE SIDES

Working into the back of each stitch to form the sides, work 60dc. Continue in dc until the sides measure approximately 3in (7cm). Cut the string to 4in (10cm) and hook the tail through the last loop. Run the tail through a few sts on the inside to finish off and trim flush .

THE LID

Using B, work 6ch and join with a sl st into a ring.
Work Rounds 1 and 2 as given for the base.
Change to A, continue Rounds 3–9 as for the base.
Now work an extra row thus:
Next round: (Dc into each of next 8 sts, 2dc into following st) 6 times (66 sts).
Work one round of dc through the back loops of the stitches only to form the sides.
Work 2 further rounds in dc.
Finish off as before .

DYEING THE BOX

Ombré dye the base of the box in tones to match or contrast with the 'dot' on the lid.

FINISHING OFF

If desired, follow the starching instructions on page 52.

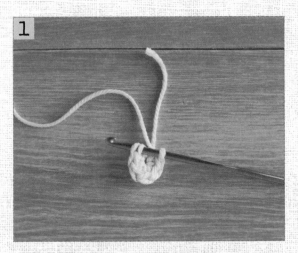

See also:

Double crochet *page 107*

Working in the round *page 112*

Increasing *page 111*

Ombré dyeing *page 70*

TIP

YOU COULD ALSO INVERT YOUR BOX
AND DYE IT FROM THE TOP DOWN.

Keep a few first-aid essentials in this practical emergency kit.
Pop it in your bag or suitcase when you're out and about.
The simple, universal motif on this purse makes it easy to
find quickly and also makes an excellent gift.

FIRST-AID PURSE

Supplies:
- [ ] 42 yards (39m) natural bakers' twine (A)
- [ ] 5 yards (5m) red bakers' twine (B)
- [ ] 3mm (UK11:US-) knitting needles
- [ ] Cream fabric for lining 8 x 15in (20 x 38cm)
- [ ] 6in (15cm) glue-in purse frame
- [ ] Fabric glue
- [ ] Sewing machine
- [ ] Sewing needle and pins
- [ ] Darning needle
- [ ] Measuring tape
- [ ] Steam iron
- [ ] Sharp scissors

Size:
6 x 6½in (15 x 16.5cm)

Tension:
9 sts x 13 rows in stocking stitch to 2in (5cm) square. Tension is important for this project to ensure the knitted piece fits the purse frame snugly.

MAIN PIECE

Using A, cast on 26 sts.

Row 1: Knit.

Row 2: Cast on 2 sts, p to end (28 sts).

Row 3: Cast on 2 sts, k to end (30 sts).

Row 4: Purl to end.

Rows 5–10: Work in stocking stitch.

Rows 11–25: Follow the chart below, using B to work the motif and stranding the yarn not in use loosely across the back of the work.

Rows 26–38: Work in stocking stitch using A.

Row 39: Cast off 3 sts, knit to end (27 sts).

Row 40: Cast off 3 sts, purl to end (24 sts).

Rows 41–46: Work in stocking stitch.

Row 47: Cast on 3 sts, knit to end (27 sts).

Row 48: Cast on 3 sts, purl to end (30 sts).

Rows 49–58: Work in stocking stitch, using A.

Rows 59–73: Follow the chart below using B to work the motif and stranding the yarn not in use loosely across the back of the work.

Rows 74–80: Work in stocking stitch.

Row 81: Cast off 3 sts, knit to end (27 sts).

Row 82: Cast off 3, purl to end (24 sts).

Row 83: Cast off loosely.

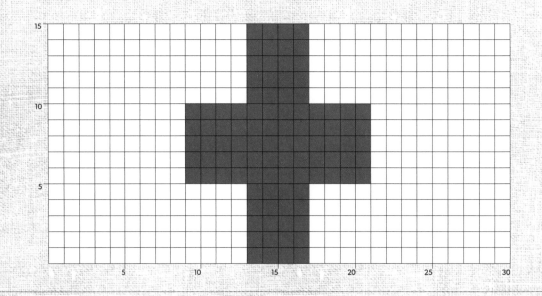

FIRST-AID PURSE CHART (15 rows x 30 sts)

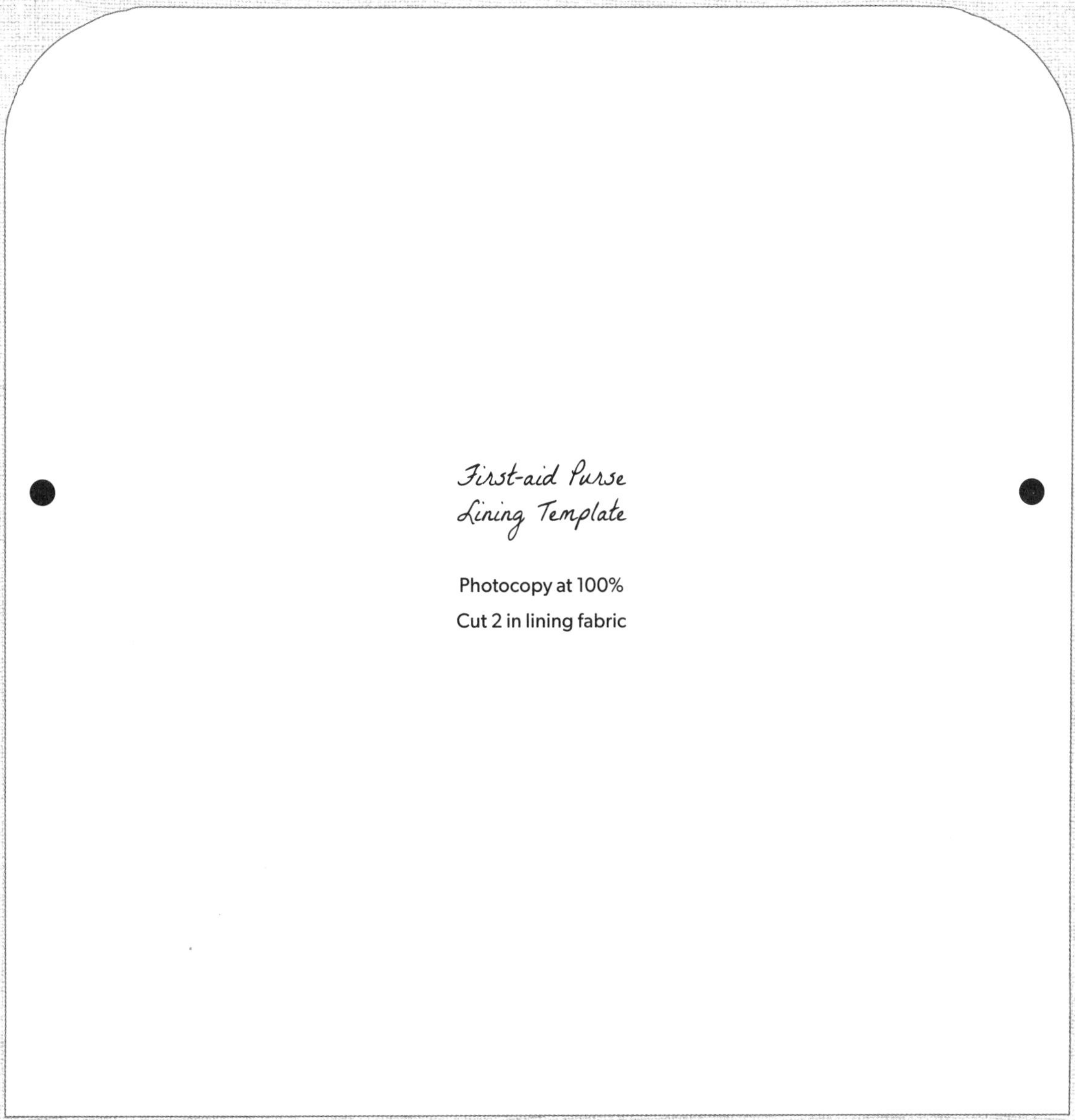

First-aid Purse
Lining Template

Photocopy at 100%

Cut 2 in lining fabric

TIP

YOU COULD MAKE A LINING IN
RIPSTOP KITE FABRIC SO THAT
THE INSIDE OF THE PURSE IS WIPE
CLEAN. A BRIGHT RED LINING
WOULD LOOK FANTASTIC.

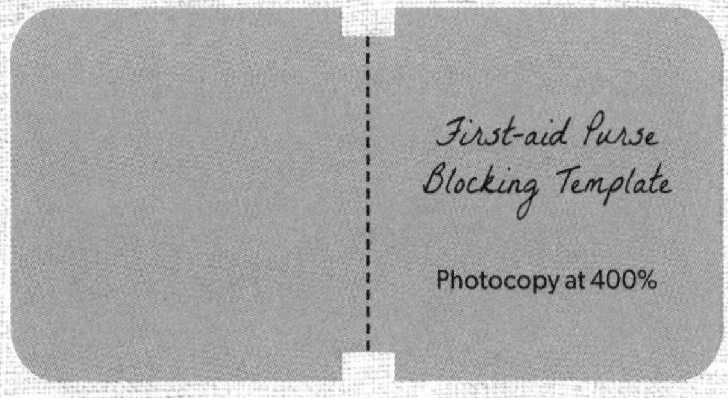

First-aid Purse
Blocking Template

Photocopy at 400%

BLOCKING THE WORK

Photocopy the blocking template on page 97 at 400% and cut it out. Pin the knitted piece to fit the template and press it using a hot steam iron **1**.

Finish off any ends by threading them on a darning needle and feeding them through the back of a few stitches at the back of the work before trimming to ⅜in (1cm) **2**.

MAKING UP THE PURSE OUTER

Fold work in half, right sides facing, across the central fold line marked on the blocking template. Align and pin or tack the two straight side edges. Machine stitch down the two sides very closely to the edge **3**.

Close the box corners by flattening them, positioning the side seams exactly on the central fold line. Align and pin or tack the two short edges together. Close the two gaps by machine sewing. Finish off all the thread ends by hand with a darning needle **4**.

MAKING THE LINING

Cut two lining pieces from cream cotton using the template on page 97. Pin together carefully, aligning the raw edges. Sew along three sides between the dots marked on the template with a seam allowance of approximately ⅜in (1cm). Reverse stitch at the beginning and end of the seam for extra strength **5**.

Press the seams open – this is fiddly, so take care not to scorch your fingers. Working on one of the bottom corners, create the flat base by making box corners. Place your hand inside the lining and push the fabric out and away from the seam. Align the side seam exactly with the bottom seam and press flat so the corner forms a triangle. Sew across 1in (2.5cm) from the point of the corner and trim the seam to ¼in (6mm) **6**.

Fold the raw top edges of the lining over and tack all the way around **7**.

ASSEMBLING THE PURSE

Turn the purse outer right side out. With the lining still inside out, place it inside the purse outer. Align all the top edges and side seams, and pin or tack in position. Sew the lining to the top edge by hand, with small overstitching **8**.

ATTACHING THE PURSE FRAME

Open the purse frame. Run a line of fabric glue along the inside of one half, beginning and ending ⅜in (1cm) from the hinge at either side. Do the same along one side of the purse opening, beginning and ending ⅜in (1cm) from each side seam. Insert the fabric in the frame, lining up the sides evenly before feeding in the centre. Use your fingers or a crochet hook to push the fabric in and make sure that the top of the outer and the lining are both hidden **9**. Leave to dry fully before gluing the other side.

See also:

Stocking stitch *page 117*
Stranding colours *page 120*
Sewn seams *page 123*

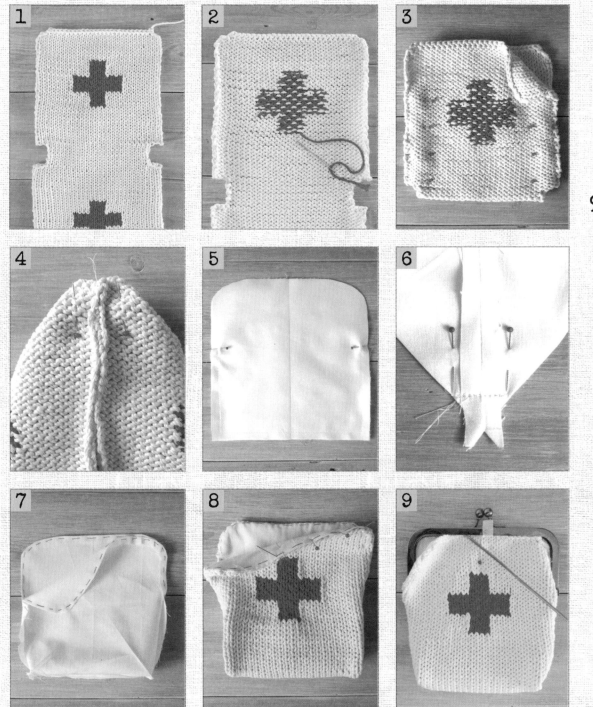

TECHNIQUES

MATERIALS AND EQUIPMENT

You will probably already have many of the items you need to make the projects in this book, and anything you don't have should be easily available. A sewing machine is useful and you will also need a steam iron and ironing board.

Some of the things you will need include:
measuring tape (1), crochet hooks (2), purse frame (3), knitting needles (double-pointed (4), circular (5) and standard (6)), lampshade (7), household string (8), cotton magicians' rope (9) or sash cord (10), polypropylene twine (11), bakers' twine (12), waxed linen thread (13), darning needle (14), sewing threads (15), scissors (16), embroidery thread (17), fabric dyes (18), tea light (19), jam jar (20), leather buckle (21).

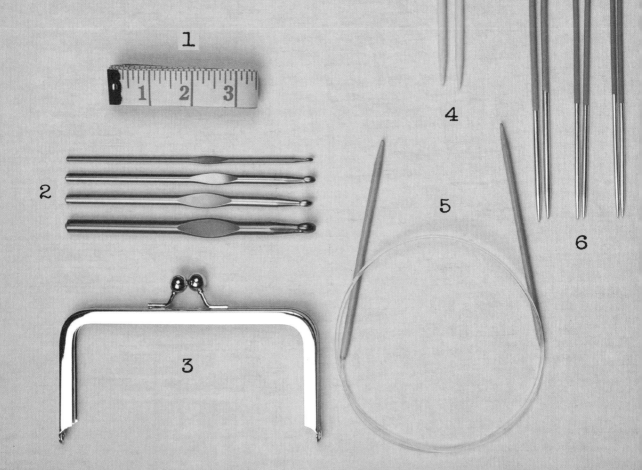

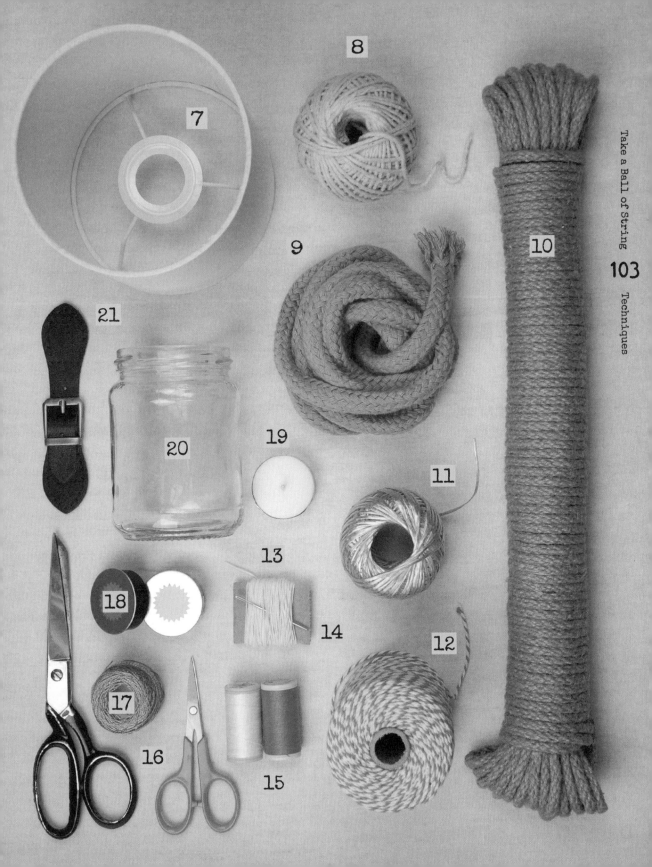

WORKING WITH STRING

Most of the string used in these patterns is beautiful bakers' twine, but butchers' twine, chunky cord and polypropylene twine all make an appearance too. In most of the projects, tension is not critical, so ordinary household string or twine, or even strong double-knitting-weight cotton may be substituted for bakers' twine. Create colourful effects by dyeing or incorporating coloured embroidery thread.

'SPINNING' YOUR STRING

String can become twisted as you work. A simple solution is to place a wide elastic band around the ball, then let it drop and spin so that it releases the twists (A).

KEEPING YOUR STRING CLOSE

Balls of string have a tendency to roll off under furniture and into dark corners while you are working. Keep them obediently at your side by capturing them in an empty bucket or wastepaper basket (B).

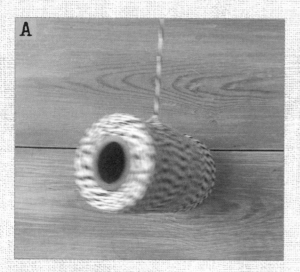

CROCHET TECHNIQUES

HOLDING THE HOOK AND YARN

Keep hold of the work and control the yarn supply with your left hand. Wrap the working yarn under the little finger, over the third finger, under the middle finger and over the index finger. Use the middle finger to feed the yarn onto the hook (A).

When you get into the rhythm of crocheting, you will develop your own way of holding the hook. I hold it in an overhand grip (B).

The instructions for these techniques are the same whether you are working with string or regular yarn.

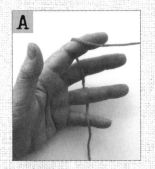

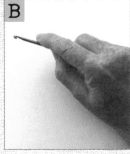

TIP

IF YOU ARE LEFT HANDED, ALL THE BASIC INSTRUCTIONS NEED TO BE FOLLOWED IN REVERSE.

MAKING A SLIP KNOT

A simple slip knot is the starting point for any piece of crochet or knitting.

Step 1
Make a loop towards the end of the yarn.

Step 2
Make a second loop and pass it through the first.

Step 3
Pull the top loop to tighten the knot and make it smaller by pulling one of the tails.

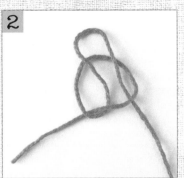

WORKING A FOUNDATION CHAIN (ch st)

Almost all crochet starts with a foundation (or base) chain, a series of stitches like casting on in knitting. From this, you can work in rows or join the chain into a ring to work in the round (see page 112).

Step 1

Make a slip knot (see page 105), insert the crochet hook into it and tighten. Hold on to the tail of the yarn with your thumb and middle finger. Wrap the ball end of the yarn clockwise over the hook.

Step 2

Catching the yarn with the hook, draw it towards and through the slip knot to make the first chain.

Step 3

Make further chains in the same way until you have the number required for your pattern. Count the stitches from the front, making sure they are not twisted. Do not count the loop currently on the hook or the initial slip knot.

SLIP STITCH (sl st)

Slip stitch is often used to join two pieces of crochet or worked along an edge to prevent it stretching.

Step 1

Insert the hook into the second chain from the hook as shown. Wrap the yarn anticlockwise over the hook.

Step 2

Pull the yarn through the chain and the loop on the hook in one movement, leaving one loop still on the hook. Work into the next chain in the same way.

WHERE TO INSERT THE HOOK

If you look closely at your crochet chains you will see that each one is made up of two 'strands' forming a V shape. You can insert the hook under either one (front or back) (**A**), or both (**B**) of the strands that make up each individual chain. Unless your pattern states otherwise, pick which suits you best, but be consistent.

DOUBLE CROCHET (dc)

Double crochet makes a taller stitch than slip stitch and creates a dense, firm fabric ideal for making items that need to hold a strong shape. Begin with a foundation chain.

Step 1

Insert the hook into both strands of the second chain from the hook. Wrap the yarn clockwise over the hook, as for slip stitch (**1a**). Pull the yarn through the chain (there are now two loops on the hook) (**1b**). Wrap yarn round hook again.

Step 2

Now draw the yarn through both loops, leaving one loop on the hook. This completes the first dc stitch.

Step 3

Insert the hook into the next stitch and repeat steps 1 and 2 to the end of the row. The hook is now at the left end of your crochet. Before starting the next row, turn your work over so that the hook is on the right again and work a turning chain (see page 108).

WORKING TURNING CHAINS

At the beginning of a follow-on row you need to work extra chains to bring the yarn up to the right height for the stitches you are about to work. These extra chains are called 'turning chains'. Without them the row would be too low at one end and your work would become uneven.

The number of chains required depends on the height of the stitch: for double crochet work one or two turning chains and for treble crochet, which is a taller stitch, work three turning chains.

Step 1

Turn work at the end of a row so that the hook is now on the right with one loop on it. Make a loose turning chain or chains by drawing a loop of yarn through the loop on the hook.

Step 2

For double crochet, work the first stitch of the row into the stitch at the base of the turning chain (2a). For treble crochet work your first stitch into the fourth stitch of the previous row (2b).

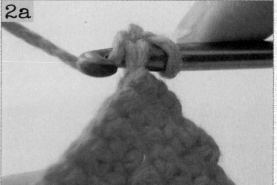

TIP

FOR DOUBLE CROCHET THE TURNING CHAIN DOES NOT COUNT AS A STITCH BUT FOR TREBLE CROCHET AND OTHER TALLER STITCHES, IT DOES.

TREBLE CROCHET (tr)

Perhaps the most commonly used stitch in crochet, treble crochet has a taller stitch than double crochet and creates a more open fabric. Work three turning chains at the beginning of follow-on rows.

Step 1

Wrap yarn over hook and insert the hook into fourth chain from hook. Wrap yarn over hook again.

Step 2

Pull the yarn through the chain, then wrap yarn over hook again.

Step 3

Pull the yarn through the first two loops only and wrap yarn over hook again.

Step 4

Pull the yarn through the last two loops on the hook (one loop remaining on hook).

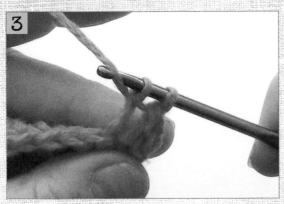

TENSION SQUARES

Working a tension square helps to guarantee the size of your finished piece. Make at least 10ch and work a minimum of 10 rows using the stitch, yarn and hook specified in your pattern. Fasten off and pin out flat, pressing if necessary using a hot iron and a damp cloth. Using a tape measure, check the number of stitches and rows to 1in (2.5cm). If there are more stitches than specified, try again with a larger hook. If there are fewer, try a smaller hook. If tension is crucial, you may have to substitute thicker or thinner string to achieve the correct count.

JOINING IN NEW YARN

Drop the old yarn just before working the final 'yarn over' of a stitch, make the yarn over using the new yarn and pull it through to complete the stitch. Hold down both tail ends until you have worked the next stitch. There is no need to knot them together.

CHANGING COLOUR

Step 1

Drop the previous colour just before working the final yarn over of a stitch, and use the new colour for the final wrap round the hook.

Step 2

Pull the yarn through so the loop on the hook is in the new colour, ready for the next stitch. Continue working in the new colour.

TIP

TO WORK A WHOLE ROW IN A NEW COLOUR, CHANGE YARN AT THE END OF THE LAST STITCH OF THE PREVIOUS ROW SO THE OLD COLOUR IS NOT CARRIED ON TO THE NEXT ROW.

INCREASING (inc)

Increases are usually made by working two or more stitches into a single stitch of the previous row:

Work the next stitch. Increase 1 st by working into the *same* stitch again – an extra stitch has now been made.

DECREASING (dec)

Decreases are made by working two or more stitches together, as follows.

Step 1

Insert the hook into the front thread only of the next two sts, then wrap the yarn round the hook.

Step 2

Pull a loop through (two loops on hook).

Step 3

Wrap the yarn round the hook again. Pull the yarn through both loops on the hook (one loop remains on hook).

TIP

INSTRUCTIONS FOR DECREASING IN
THE MIDDLE OF A ROW ARE USUALLY
GIVEN WITHIN THE PATTERN.

WORKING IN THE ROUND

Step 1

Work a foundation chain with the required number of chains (see page 106). Join into a ring by inserting the hook into the first ch, wrapping yarn and pulling through to make a slip stitch.

Step 2

To work the stitches for the first round, insert the hook into the centre of the ring. At the beginning of each subsequent round make a turning chain (see page 108).

Step 3

From the second round, insert the hook under the top two loops of the stitches in the previous round, unless the pattern states otherwise. Follow the pattern instructions to increase as required.
Do not turn your work between rounds.

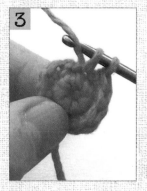

Step 4

At the end of each round, insert the hook into the top of the starting chain and slip stitch to join into a round again. Work a turning chain as in Step 2.

Note: Some patterns are worked in a spiral. In this case, omit the 'turning chain' and follow the pattern instructions for increasing as you work.

FINISHING OFF

Step 1

Make 1ch and cut the working yarn leaving a 2–4in (5–10cm) tail. Pull the tail through the loop and tighten to prevent unravelling.

Step 2

Use a yarn needle or small crochet hook to weave the tail through the stitches at the back of your work. Cut the tail flush using sharp scissors.

KNITTING TECHNIQUES

HOLDING THE NEEDLES AND YARN

There is no right or wrong way to hold the needles and yarn; you will find what is most comfortable for you as your confidence builds. These suggestions may help beginners.

Hold the right-hand needle between the thumb and index finger, and curl your third and fourth fingers loosely over the needle to hold it against your palm. Hold the left-hand needle lightly from above, using the thumb and index finger to control the tip (A).

Hold the yarn in the right hand and pass under the little finger, over the third finger, under the centre finger and over the index finger (B). Pass the yarn round the needle tip using your index finger. Control the tension by gripping the yarn in the crook of your little finger. In time you will develop a rhythm, moving your index finger to wind the yarn around the needle point for each stitch while at the same time letting it run through your hand at the correct tension.

The instructions for these techniques are the same whether you are working with string or regular yarn.

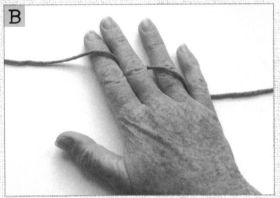

TIP

SOME PEOPLE LIKE TO HOLD THE YARN IN THEIR LEFT HAND IN A SIMILAR WAY TO WHEN CROCHETING (SEE PAGE 105).

Step 1
Make a slip knot (see page 105), place it on the left needle. This will count as your first stitch.

Step 2
Insert the tip of the right-hand needle through the slip knot. Wrap the yarn round to the back and between the two needles, bringing it to the front.

Step 3
Pull a loop through from the back to the front on to the right-hand needle.

Step 4
Transfer the loop to the left-hand needle (4a). There are now two stitches on the left-hand needle (4b).

Step 5
* Insert the right-hand needle between the two stitches on the left-hand needle. Wind the yarn round the point of the right-hand needle. Draw a loop through and place on the left-hand needle. Continue from * until the required number of sts have been cast on.

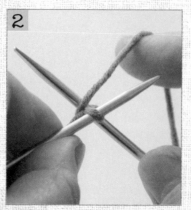

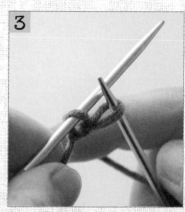

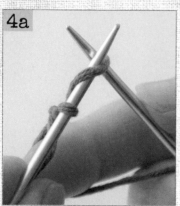

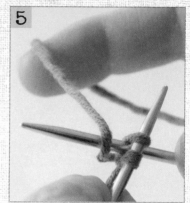

KNIT STITCH (k)

Step 1
With the yarn at the back of the work, insert the right-handle needle from left to right through the front of the first stitch on the left-handle needle.

Step 2
Wind the yarn round the right-hand needle to the front.

Step 3
Pull a loop through from the back to the front.

Step 4
Slip the original stitch off the left-hand needle.

Repeat until all stitches have been transferred from the left-hand to the right-hand needle.

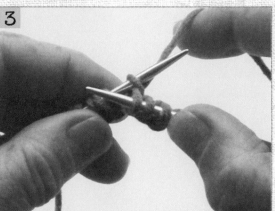

PURL STITCH (p)

Step 1
With the yarn at the front of the work, insert the right-hand needle from right to left through the front of the first stitch on the left-hand needle.

Step 2
Wind the yarn round the right-hand needle.

Step 3
Draw a loop through to the back.

Step 4
Slip the original stitch off the left-hand needle.

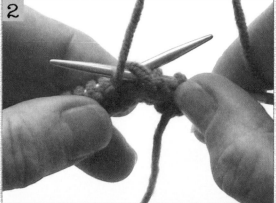

TENSION SQUARE

Working a tension square helps to guarantee the size of your finished piece. Cast on at least 10 stitches and work a minimum of 10 rows in stocking stitch (see below). Cast off and pin flat, then press with a steam iron. Measure the number of stitches and rows to 1in (2.5cm). If there are more than specified in the pattern, try again using larger needles. If there are fewer, try smaller needles. If tension is crucial, you may have to use thicker or thinner string to achieve the correct stitch count.

GARTER STITCH

This is formed by working every row as a knit row. The first row is usually the right side. The same effect can be achieved by working every row as a purl row.

STOCKING STITCH

This is formed by working the first and every odd row in knit stitch, and the second and every even row in purl stitch. The first row is usually the right side. The resulting work is smooth on one side (A) and bumpy like garter stitch on the reverse (B).

MOSS OR SEED STITCH

This forms a textured pattern that lies flat and does not curl at the edges. For the first row, k1, p1 to the end. For the second row, knit the purl stitches and purl the knit stitches.

METHODS FOR INCREASING

INCREASE 1 IN NEXT ST (inc 1 or inc)
Usually used at the beginning and end of a row and involves working twice into the same stitch.

On a knit row, knit into the front of the stitch as usual, then knit into the back of the same stitch (**A**) before slipping it off the needle (**B**).

On a purl row, purl into the front of the stitch, then purl into the back of the same stitch before slipping it off the needle.

MAKE 1 (M1)
This increase is used in the middle of a row.

Step 1
Pick up the loop between the stitch on the needle and the next stitch.

Step 2
Place the loop on the left-hand needle and knit into the back of it to create an extra stitch.

YARN OVER NEEDLE (yon) OR YARN FORWARD (yf)
This increase leaves a visible hole and is often used in lacy patterns.

On a knit row (yf), knit a stitch, bring the yarn to the front, take it over the right-hand needle and knit the next stitch (**A**).

On a purl row (yon), take the yarn over the right-hand needle to the back of the work, then under the needle to the front (**B**).

METHODS FOR DECREASING

WORK TWO STITCHES TOGETHER
(k2tog or p2tog)
This creates a right-hand sloping stitch on the knit side of your work.

On a knit row, insert the right-hand needle through two stitches instead of one (A). Knit them together as if they were one stitch (B).

On a purl row, insert the needle purlwise through the two stitches (C). Purl in the usual way (D).

WORK TWO STITCHES TOGETHER THROUGH THE BACK LOOPS (k2tog tbl or p2tog tbl)
This produces a left-sloping stitch on the front of the work.

On a knit row, insert the right-hand needle knitwise through the back loops of the next two stitches on the left-hand needle (A). Knit them as if they were one stitch (B).

On a purl row (p2tog tbl), insert the right-hand needle purlwise through the back loops. Purl them as if they were one stitch.

SLIP ONE, KNIT ONE, PASS SLIPPED STITCH OVER (skpo)
This also creates a left-sloping stitch on the front of the work.

Slip the next stitch on to the right-hand needle as if to knit it. Knit the next stitch. Lift the slipped stitch over the knitted stitch (A) and drop it off the needle (B).

On a purl row (sppo), slip one, purl one, pass slipped stitch over.

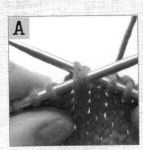
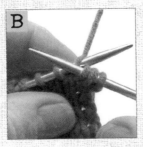

JOINING IN A NEW BALL OF YARN

It is best to join new yarn at the beginning of a row. To join in the middle of a row, just pick up the new yarn and continue knitting. Work a few more rows, then weave the tails of the old and new yarns into the back of the work using a large tapestry needle or a small crochet hook (see Finishing ends, opposite).

STRANDING COLOURS (A)
When two or more colours are used on the same row, carry the yarn not in use loosely across the wrong side of work. To work the second colour, exchange the yarn and continue. To avoid long loops of yarn at the back of your work when working a run of stitches, twist the yarns together every two or three stitches.

WORKING BLOCKS OF COLOUR (B)
For large areas of one colour, use a separate ball of yarn for each block of colour, rather than stranding the yarn across the row. Twist the yarns when changing colour to prevent holes. If the colour change is in a vertical line, cross the yarns on every row. If it is on a slant, cross on alternate rows.

> **TIP**
>
> DO NOT KNOT YARNS IN THE MIDDLE OF A ROW AS THEY WILL FORM A BUMP THAT SHOWS ON THE RIGHT SIDE.

> **TIP**
>
> DO NOT PULL THE YARN NOT IN USE TOO TIGHTLY WHEN CHANGING COLOUR, OR YOUR WORK MAY PUCKER.

CASTING OFF

This is used to finish off your work securely.
When casting off a piece of stocking stitch, cast off
knitwise on a knit row or purlwise on a purl row.
When casting off a piece worked in a pattern,
cast off using the same stitches as the pattern.

CASTING OFF KNITWISE

Step 1
Knit the first two stitches in the usual way so that
there are two stitches on the right-hand needle.
Insert the tip of the left-hand needle into the first
stitch on the right-hand needle.

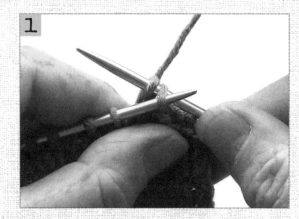

Step 2
* Lift the first stitch over the second stitch and drop
it off the needle, leaving one stitch remaining on
the right-hand needle. Knit the next stitch from the
left-hand needle. Repeat from * as required.

CASTING OFF PURLWISE
Purl the first two stitches. *Using the left-hand
needle, lift the first stitch over the second (one stitch
on needle). Purl the next stitch and repeat from *.

If casting off all stitches, cut yarn leaving a tail after
the last stitch and pull through the final stitch.

FINISHING ENDS (A)
Use a darning needle or crochet hook to weave
the tail of yarn through the back of several stitches,
then cut the end flush.

JOINING PIECES OF KNITTING

GRAFTING (KITCHENER STITCH)
To join two pieces of work invisibly, do not cast off at the end of your work.

Step 1
Thread a darning needle with a length of yarn. Place the pieces to be joined right sides facing and hold the knitting needles in your left hand.

Step 2
Pass the darning needle knitwise through the first stitch on the front knitting needle and slide the stitch off the needle.

Step 3
Pass the darning needle purlwise through the second stitch on the same needle, leaving it on the needle.

Step 4
Now pass the darning needle purlwise through the first stitch on the back knitting needle and slide the stitch off the needle.

Step 5
Pass the darning needle knitwise through the second stitch on the back knitting needle, leaving the stitch on the needle.

Step 6
Repeat from Step 2, teasing and tweaking the yarn as you work so the stitches match the knitted ones. Darn in the ends.

SEWN SEAMS

When working with cotton thread, yarn or string that have little elasticity, you can join straight or simple seams by machine. First, pin or tack the edges right sides together, then sew. Reverse stitch at either end for extra strength.

If you have no sewing machine, join the seams by hand using a darning needle and mattress stitch (A).

PICKING UP STITCHES

ALONG A CAST-ON OR CAST-OFF EDGE (A)
Insert the point of the needle under the first stitch, pass the yarn round the needle and draw a loop through to form a stitch. Repeat as required.

ALONG SIDE EDGES (B)
With the right side of the work facing, insert the point of the needle between the first and second rows, one whole stitch in from the edge. Pass yarn over the needle and draw the loop through. The number of stitches to be picked up is usually less than the number of rows worked. A good tip is to divide the length of the edge into eighths, marking each section using pins. Then divide the number of stitches to be picked up by eight so you know roughly how many to pick up across each section.

TIP

ALWAYS PICK UP A WHOLE STITCH, NEVER A SINGLE THREAD.

MAKING AN I-CORD

A basic i-cord makes excellent hanging loops or handles. You can also make a joined-on i-cord by picking up stitches as you work. This is a good way to finish a cast-on or cast-off edge, or create a border or edge across a seam.

BASIC I-CORD

Using short double-pointed needles, cast on an odd number of stitches, in this case five.

Row 1: *K5, push sts to other end of needle but do not turn. Bring yarn firmly round back of sts ready to work the next row.

Repeat from * to required length. Cast off, leaving a tail for finishing.

JOINED-ON I-CORD

Step 1
Using double-pointed needles, or a very short circular needle, cast on 5 sts. K4, sl1. Insert the right-hand needle through a stitch from the top edge of the work where you want the i-cord to start.

Step 2
Wrap yarn round the needle and draw a stitch through. There are now 6 sts on the needle.

Step 3
Using the left-hand needle, pass the slipped stitch over the picked-up stitch (5 sts). Do not turn.

Step 4
Push sts to the other end of the needle and bring yarn firmly across the back of the work. Repeat steps to the desired length for your i-cord.

Crochet abbreviations

alt	alternate	**foll**	following	**sl st**	slip stitch
beg	beginning	**inc**	increase	**st(s)**	stitch(es)
bet	between	**mm**	millimetres	**tr**	treble crochet
cm	centimetres	**rem**	remain(ing)	**ws**	wrong side
dc	double crochet	**rep**	repeat		
dec	decrease	**rs**	right side		

Knitting abbreviations

alt	alternate	**m1**	make one stitch	**skpo**	slip 1, knit 1, pass slipped stitch over
beg	beginning	**m**	metre		
bet	between	**mm**	millimetres	**sl**	slip
cm	centimetres	**p**	purl	**st(s)**	stitch(es)
dec	decrease	**p2tog**	purl two stitches together	**st st**	stocking stitch
dpn	double-pointed needle			**tbl**	through the back of the loop
foll	following	**psso**	pass slipped stitch over		
in(s)	inch(es)			**ws**	wrong side
inc	increase	**rem**	remain(ing)	**yds**	yards
k	knit	**rep**	repeat	**yon**	yarn over needle
k2tog	knit two stitches together	**rev st st**	reverse stocking stitch		
		rs	right side		

Conversions

KNITTING NEEDLES

UK	Metric	US
11	3mm	–
8	4mm	6
6	5mm	8
4	6mm	10

CROCHET HOOKS

UK	Metric	US
12	2.5mm	C/2
11	3mm	_
9	3.5mm	E/4
8	4mm	G/6
7	4.5mm	7
6	5mm	H/8
000	10mm	N–P-15

CROCHET TERMS

UK	US
dc double crochet	**sc** single crochet
tr treble (tr)	**dc** double crochet

Suppliers

STRING, TWINE AND ROPE
James Lever
www.jameslever.co.uk

James Lever was established in 1856. Cotton
bindings collected from mills around Bolton
were transformed into sturdy rope and sold
back to the mills as transmission ropes. As mill
machinery became more sophisticated, Levers
branched out into manufacturing a diverse range
of products including plaited cords, twines and
sash cords. Today, with over 150 years' experience
of manufacturing ropes, James Lever supply a wide
range of string and twine products across the UK,
throughout Europe and the world. I would like to
express my gratitude for their support in supplying
me with their beautiful strings, twines and ropes.

PURSE CLIPS AND LEATHER BUCKLES
Bag-clasps
www.bag-clasps.co.uk

EMBROIDERY AND SEWING THREADS
Coates Crafts
www.makeitcoates.co.uk

LAMPSHADE
B&Q
www.diy.com

LIQUID STARCH
Walmart
www.walmart.com

DYES
Dylon
www.dylon.co.uk

Acknowledgements

AUTHOR'S ACKNOWLEDGEMENTS
Thank you to Jonathan, Gilda, Virginia, Luana and
everyone at GMC who helped in the production
of this book, to Andrew Perris for the lovely location
photographs, Martha for the hand shots and Mop
for her critical eye. As always, the most thanks to
my family and my friends. Thank you all x

GMC PUBLICATIONS would like to thank:
Georgina Holt at Sandways in Camber Sands,
for allowing us to photograph the projects there,
Utility, Brighton for the loan of props and James
Lever for providing us with lots of lovely string.

Index

Page numbers in bold contain photographs of the completed projects.

To place an order, or to request
a catalogue, contact:

GMC Publications Ltd, Castle Place,
166 High Street, Lewes, East Sussex,
BN7 1XU, United Kingdom

Tel: +44 (0)1273 488005
www.gmcbooks.com